"Any Grooming Hints for Your Fans, Rollie?"

D0783376

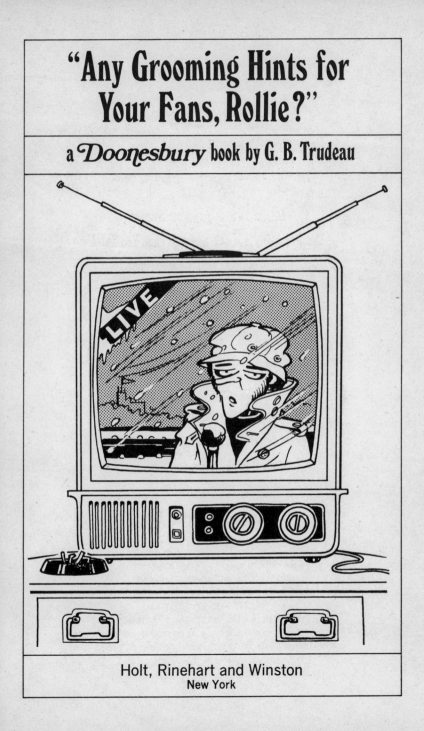

"Any Grooming Hints for Your Fans, Rollie?"

a *Doonesbury* book by G. B. Trudeau

Holt, Rinehart and Winston
New York

Copyright © 1977, 1978 by G. B. Trudeau
All rights reserved, including the right to reproduce
this book or portions thereof in any form.
Published simultaneously in Canada by Holt, Rinehart
and Winston of Canada, Limited.
Library of Congress Catalog Card Number: 78-53781
ISBN: 0-03-044861-1
Printed in the United States of America
The cartoons in this book have appeared in newspapers
in the United States and abroad under the auspices of
Universal Press Syndicate.

10   9   8   7   6   5   4   3   2   1

LAETRILE? YOU'RE GOING INTO THE LAETRILE BUSINESS?
BITE YOUR TONGUE, NEPHEW! OF COURSE NOT! LAETRILE'S STILL ILLEGAL IN THIS STATE!
ALL I'M DOING IS BUYING INTO A LITTLE APRICOT FARM! AND IF I JUST HAPPEN TO FIND A MARKET FOR MY PITS IN TIJUANA, WHO COULD BLAME ME FOR SELLING THEM?
UNCLE DUKE, THAT'S JUST AWFUL! HOW COULD YOU EVEN CONSIDER SUCH A SCHEME!
I SUPPOSE I WOULD BE REMISS IF I FAILED TO MENTION THE 600% PROFIT MARGIN.
DUKE, THE STUFF DOESN'T EVEN WORK ON RATS!
THEY'RE NOT BUYING. WHY DO YOU ALWAYS GET SO TICKED WHEN I THINK OF SOMETHING FIRST?
GBTrudeau

BACK ALREADY?
YUP! THE CLOSING WAS A PIECE OF CAKE!
WITH JULIO ACTING AS PRESIDENT, THE MINORITY SMALL BUSINESS LOAN CAME THROUGH! THE "SHADY GROVES" APRICOT FARM IS MINE!
AND JUST WHAT DOES OL' JULIO GET OUT OF ALL THIS?
2% AND A GREEN CARD.
OH, DUKE...
HEY, I HAD TO DO SOMETHING! HE'S GOT EIGHT LITTLE WETBACKS TO FEED!
GBTrudeau

DUKE, YOU'RE LUCKY THAT COP HAD A SENSE OF HUMOR! WHAT WERE YOU DOING UP IN THAT TREE?
HIDING FROM THE KILLER SHEEP! WHAT DO YOU THINK?!
KILLER SHEEP? I THOUGHT YOU WERE TALKING TO THE YOUNG REPUBLICANS!
I HAD 'EM UNDER CONTROL RIGHT UP TO THE END! BUT WHEN I OPENED THE FLOOR UP TO QUESTIONS, THEY ALL STARTED BLEATING, "WE WANT GOLDWATER! WE WANT GOLDWATER!"
AND?..
WELL, NATURALLY, I PANICKED.
G B Trudeau

AFTER IT WAS ALL OVER, TEDDY WAS LEFT WITH A SERIOUS WORLD OPINION PROBLEM! SO HE PRESSED HIS ATTORNEY-GENERAL, PHILANDER KNOX, TO DEFEND THE U.S. ACTION IN PANAMA!
KNOX DEMURRED. "MR. PRESIDENT," HE WROTE, "DO NOT LET SO GREAT AN ACHIEVEMENT SUFFER FROM ANY TAINT OF LEGALITY!"
HEY, Z! HOW COME YOU KNOW ALL THIS PANAMA STUFF ANYWAY?
BRIEFING BOOKS, KIRBY! WHEN I WAS IN SAMOA A FEW YEARS BACK, MY UNCLE DUKE WAS WORKING ON A PLAN TO ANNEX IT!
ANNEX THE CANAL? REALLY?
SURE! IT'S INDEFENSIBLE, YOU KNOW!
OH, WOW! IS YOUR UNCLE DUKE A GENERAL OR SOMETHING?
GB Trudeau

ACTUALLY, KIRBY, THE MOST AMAZING THING ABOUT THE CANAL IS THAT THEY FINISHED IT A YEAR AHEAD OF SCHEDULE!
REALLY?
UH-HUH! NOT ONLY THAT, BUT IT ALSO COST SEVERAL MILLION **LESS** THAN IT WAS SUPPOSED TO!
WHAT HAPPENED? SOME SORT OF ACCOUNTING ERROR?
NO, THEY REALLY BROUGHT IT IN UNDER BUDGET!
HMM.. SOUNDS LIKE ROOSEVELT WAS TRYING TO SCORE SOME NEEDED POINTS!
OH, ABSOLUTELY! SEE, THE SPANISH-AMERICAN WAR WENT WAY OVER BUDGET..
I DIDN'T THINK THAT WAS HIS PROJECT..
©GB Trudeau

HEY, PARTNER!
ROLAND! ROLAND BURTON HEDLEY, JR! LONG TIME, MAN! WHAT ARE YOU DOING HERE?
ON A GIG! I'M WORKING FOR ABC NEWS NOW! DOING A MINI-DOCUMENTARY ON THIS YEAR'S CAMPUS MOOD!
AHA! THE EVER POPULAR STATE-OF-THE-STUDENT STORY!
RIGHT! I WAS OUT AT YOUR COMMUNE, AND MARK TOLD ME YOU AND MIKE WERE LIVING ON CAMPUS NOW!
YEAH, WE MOVED INTO THE DORM LAST WEEK!
WHAT IS THIS, SOME SORT OF TREND?
UH-HUH. WE GOT THE IDEA FROM "TIME."
GBTrudeau

ZONKER HARRIS IS A VETERAN COLLEGE STUDENT WITH HIS EAR TO THE GROUND. TELL ME, ZONKER, WHAT'S THE SCENE LIKE TODAY? ARE KIDS STILL "TURNING ON" AND "TUNING OUT"?
abc
THEY CERTAINLY ARE, ROLAND, AND IN EVER-GROWING NUMBERS! WHILE THE USE OF "ACID" IS DOWN, OTHER STAPLES SUCH AS "GRASS" AND "COKE" HAVE REGISTERED IMPRESSIVE GAINS!
abc
HOWEVER, BY THE END OF THE YEAR, I'D LOOK FOR MORE "DOWNERS" AND I THINK YOU'LL FIND MANY STUDENTS WILL BE MOVING TOWARD THE MORE TRADITIONAL CENTRAL NERVOUS SYSTEM DEPRESSANTS!
abc
YOU MEAN.. ALCOHOL?!
RIGHT. THE KIDS CALL IT "GETTING PLASTERED" OR "BOMBED."
abc